Writing For Success

Goldmine Tips On How To Write Articles Fast, How To Create Top Quality Products and How To Write Great Copy

Ioan Draniciar

Copyright 2012

Table of Contents

How to Write an Article in 7 Minutes 3

How to Create a Top Quality Information Product in 2 Hours or Less 6

How to Master a Skill That Can Make You $10,000 per Month for Just a Few Hours a Day 16

Final Words 26

Other Books Written by Ioan Draniciar 27

How to Write an Article in 7 Minutes

If you want to learn how to crank up articles pretty fast and easy then you came to the right place. I've learned this method from a fellow internet marketer named Cory Friedman.

This article writing formula is designed to help you overcome writer's block and start writing articles pretty fast and easy. Such style of writing isn't perfect but it will make you take action and get the job done.

With practice you can write articles a lot easier and faster. Write at your own pace. Knowing how to structure your article is what helps and matters the most.

The idea is to stop procrastinating and take action. This method has been proven to work very well for those who have used it. Some people will complain others will take action.

To be honest, most of you won't be able to write an article so quickly from the start. It takes practice to get there but once you know how to structure an article, things become a lot easier.

The research for information that is needed to write an article is not included in the 7 minutes time span.

You should have gathered already interesting and useful information related to your topic. Once you've done your research, it's time to write the article.

The structure of an article is pretty simple: introduction, 3 main points and conclusion. Here is a very short written version of the article writing formula:

1. Introduction paragraph

a. Attention grabbing opener (If, then is always effective). Example: "If you want to learn how to make money online then you should read this post carefully."

b. Overview of 3 main points you'll be covering.

c. Tell them what they are going to accomplish by reading the article. This is your hook - you're making sure they remain interested by telling them how they are going to benefit from reading your article.

2. The 3 main points A, B and C. For each main point you'll write the following:

a. General statement about main point

b. Specific statement about main point

c. Sub-point #1 that backs up specific statement

d. sub-point #2 that backs up specific statement

e. Transition to the next main point paragraph

3. Conclusion paragraph

a. General statement

b. Re-iterate the main points

c. Tell the reader what they can now do with the information. Example: "Now you have the wisdom and the power to write good articles pretty fast and build a great online reputation that will help you make more money for years to come."

d. Resource box: let the readers know about you and the benefits they'll get if they visit your site.

How to Create a Top Quality Information Product in 2 Hours or Less

I'll start with a little disclaimer here. I've learned this product creation technique by watching one of Jason Fladlien's webinars and I can honestly say that this is one of the most incredible content I've seen in 2012 so far. Using the methods I am about to show you, Jason Fladlien made 2 million dollars from March 1st 2011 until February 2012. With that out of the way, let's get started.

In the short term, a mediocre product with good marketing will make you more money than a good product with mediocre marketing. This is true for the short term but not so much in the long run. Over time, good products will start to almost market themselves as long as you can get some customers with your mediocre marketing because in the long run your customers will be a lot more interested in your products and it will be a lot easier to sell to them. On top of that they will be interested in recommending and promoting a good product for you.

You don't need proof to successfully sell information products online. Proof can help but is not required. Proof usually makes the difference between five figure products and six figure products. But eventually you will get proof as they buy your product which will push your product to six or even seven figure results.

Many people say that most good product ideas have already being taken. That is false!

Every day technology evolves and new opportunities that previously didn't exist are now available to product creators. Look at how many information products have been created around Facebook, Kindle or Pinterest. Pinterest is very hot right now and everybody is talking about how much money you can make on Pinterest. I bet there is something being created right this very moment that will be a go to product in the future and you could create an information course around it and make sales.

Speed is more important than ever for product creation. I am going to show you how to create top quality information products in 2 hours or less that automatically can generate traffic and convert with subpar marketing. The product has to be top quality if you want to make it the easiest way in the world to make money.

Here's the product creation formula that helped Jason make his 1st dollar online and millions later on: <u>1 sitting, 1 problem, 1 solution product creation!</u> "If ever there was anything to write down, this is it!" But don't just write this down, you need to memorize it, you need to tattoo this on your mind, dream about it and wake up in the morning doing it!

1 SITTING, ONE PROBLEM, 1 SOLUTION PRODUCT CREATION!

From his experience Jason realized that if he gave himself a week, he could not finish creating a product. If he gave himself 2 days, he still could not finish creating the product!

The same result with 24 hours time limit, he still could not finish the product! In fact, if he stopped at any point when he first sat down to create a product, he could not finish it!

THE SOLUTION

The product creation starts when you sit down and begin working on it and the product is FINISHED when you get up! Someone asked 'What if I got to go to the bathroom?' Well there are really only two options available to you: you either hurry up to finish the product or you hold it. This is how serious you need to be when it comes to this stuff. You sit down and start, when you get out of that chair you've finished! Whether it's an info product, an audio or a video, this is what you have to do this is the goal, the formula!

Jason sits down looking at a blank screen and he gets up with something that made him thousands of dollars every single time, usually tens of thousands of dollars and sometimes even hundreds of thousands of dollars.

What does this mean? Your product must be short, must be actionable, must cover the essentials, in other words you don't do anybody any favors by taking 50 minutes to explain something that could be said in 5 minutes. For some people it takes 50 minutes to explain something that could be done in 5 minutes because they allow themselves too much time to create the product but when you have the clock set up for a 2 hour window or when you sit down and when you get up the product is finished, you have to get right to the point.

This is great for your customers because they don't have to sit through the fluff, they can get right on with it and get some benefit out of it immediately! It's good for them and it's good for you to be able to create immediately good quality products. You don't have to spend so much of your time to make that money!

The product must be short and actionable. Actionable means step-by-step: first do this, second do that and so on until the problem is solved. Your product has to cover the essentials which means you can't start with the basics, the boring stuff; you can't start with the history. You just get to the point and say 'Hey, if you want to do this then start here, go!'

The average person who is purchasing info products is not used to get value like that so they immediately are going to love your stuff if you can present it within these parameters. So don't present them history lessons, don't try to anticipate every possible scenario, don't cover the minutia, no big grandiose solutions; provide them one solution for one problem and not one problem, fifty solutions! You need to focus on one problem and provide the best solution for it and don't try to cover 50 different things.

If you follow this formula so tightly focused on solving just one problem, it will be a lot easier to market even if you're not that good at marketing because you're so tightly focused on covering a very specific segment and solving a very specific problem.

You're immediately getting the attention from somebody who suffers from that problem and they are going to be even more likely to buy your stuff because it's so tailor made to them. Thus way you automatically improve your marketing without even trying to improve your marketing. You create products in one sitting that focus on solving one problem with one solution!

It might be a little bit of a challenge, it might push you a bit but with practice I think we can all do it. It does not have to be perfect but make sure it's good. You don't have too much to lose since it didn't take you that long to create it.

Anyone who has a good amount of desire, some ambition and a bit of focus can do this. You don't have to be Superman to make it happen. You got to want it and be willing to put in some work if you're willing to make some real money. You need to have the focus to work two hours here, two hours there in order to make it work. Desire is the most important. You really have to desire your wealth! You can be the smartest person in the world but without desire you won't accomplish anything! Even if you have a below average intelligence but have all the desire, guess what, it can change your life.

So when you create a product you need to follow this path:

1. One problem, one solution, one sitting.
2. Presented in step by step format.
3. Sold at a ridiculously low price!

Now you're probably asking yourself why sell your product at such a ridiculously low price. You might of thought that you have to sell at such a low price to build a list and if you thought of that, that would be incorrect. It is a secondary benefit but that's not the main reason. If that's not the reason then maybe it is to make sales. That's true, you will make money but that's still not the main reason. Maybe it is because you want to establish some authority, get a reputation, speed up that process. You can do all those things for sure but that's still not the main reason.

The reason why you have to sell it at a ridiculously low price is because it takes all the pressure off! There is no pressure when you sit down to create a product that will sell for a couple bucks. Guess what pressure invites in: procrastination! Pressure leads to procrastination. On the other hand, with lack of pressure, no pressure at all, you just get it done! So you need to do this just to get it done, get it out there and start making money. That way you'll see that it's possible. Think about it like having a giant check in your brain waiting to be translated into cash.

You can agonize over potential success inviting in procrastination or you can understand that success is inevitable.

Here's the inevitable success:

1. If the product sells well, great! You will be financially successful immediately.
2. If it doesn't sell well, great! Who cares if it does not sell well? First of all it only took you a couple hours to create it.

3. You can use the product that doesn't sell well to leverage it, to make everything else you do in the future infinitely easier to make money with. For example you can take that product and offer it as a free bonus to the next product you create. That way it would be a lot easier to sell that product. Or you can take that product and offer it as a bonus when you're promoting affiliate offers. You can also take that product and offer it in exchange for an email address and build your list. You can chop that product up and create multiple articles you can use to submit to article directories in order to create backlinks and get more traffic to your site. You can take those articles and create videos to submit to YouTube and other video directories. You can leverage that product several ways to make money easier in the future.
4. If it does ok, great! Because it does not take so many ok products to build a six figure income.

This is inevitable success if you truly get this and not just intellectually. If you truly get this it will alter your behavior and you will actually do it and you will truly embrace inevitable success and you will become inevitably successful!

Try to create the best value products you possibly can within these parameters. Not all your products will be home runs but with experience, eventually some of them will get to that level.

Before you reach that level it is just as important to understand what not to do. So here's what you should not do:

- You're not going to be able to hit a home run trying to sell something to somebody that does not want it.

- Don't compete in niches that are way too big, against big corporations because they have a way bigger budget than you. It's like jumping up and down in the ocean and the ocean would not even notice it. You're going to drown in the ocean even trying to make one sale. You can make six or seven figures a year easy by jumping up and down in puddles.

There are lots of puddles and only four oceans!

- Don't create products you can't do in one sitting.

- You can't create products to sell to people who don't have any money to buy them in the first place. Take teenagers for example. You can create a 'how to make money for teenagers' product but they don't have a credit card to purchase it.

- Some niches are too small to be worth creating a product.

This is how to do it right:

1. Create instant gratification products.
2. Create products in one sitting.
3. Solve it with one solution to one problem.

Most people focus on the big benefit when selling info products. That may not be the best way to do it. Handling problems and focusing on the problems and the pain they currently experience and creating products that solve the pain that people immediately and currently experiencing and are desperate for a solution, these are the products that people are going to be far more willing to pay money for than the products that only focus on big benefits.

Benefits are something that you can enjoy in the future but you currently don't enjoy. Problems, pains are things you currently experience that you would like to not experience them in the future.

A product that focuses on addressing immediate pain with a fast solution is going to do far better than the benefit only products. If you really get that, all of a sudden opportunities start popping up and you will now unconsciously have online radar to show you how to create one problem, one solution products.

Products that can show the customer how to solve a problem in less time and with far better results are going to do very well.

This is like when you buy a car and all of a sudden you start noticing all the similar cars because you own one. It is called awareness and this is what you should have from now on.

The easiest path to creating six figure products:

Create a 1-1-1 product that...

- Promises a specific solution in a specific time frame

- Solves an "immediate problem with less effort required!

How to Master a Skill That Can Make You $10,000 per Month for Just a Few Hours a Day

Copywriting is an ancient art of persuasion and is all about words and how you lay them out so people understand the value of the offer you're presenting and then hopefully the most amount of them take the quickest action possible. It's the ability to transform something that does not exist into something that can make profit and do so in hopefully 90 minutes or less.

Copywriting is an essential skill for internet marketers and is in demand more than ever with new info products, advertising platforms, email auto responders showing up every day on the market. So what we have is more demand than ever and less quality copywriters out there right now.

I was inspired to write this article by watching a free webinar done by one of the greatest copywriters of our time, Jason Fladlien. Jason made over 2.5 million dollars by using copywriting. He admitted that if he didn't know copywriting, he probably would have made only 5 percent of those $2.5 million.

In this article I am going to show you how by focusing only on 3 things you can create great copy in less than 2 hours.

You can do this for products or services that you previously didn't know a single thing about, find out what the product is, write the copy for it and have it go live in less than 90 minutes and earn up to $30,000 for that effort.

How do you do that? You focus on 3 things only:

1. **Headline**
2. **Offer**
3. **Urgency**

"A headline is 80 cents of your dollar". A good headline will keep four out of five people reading your message. However a bad headline will immediately lose four out of five people. Four out of five people will decide in less than 10 seconds whether they are going to stay or leave the page so you need to get the headline right or you'll lose 80 percent of your audience.

Headlines do not sell anything; headlines just get the prospects to continue to stay on the page and hopefully read the offer. Then the offer convinces them whether to buy or not. So the question is how can we position the offer so that the highest number of people would get excited and say yes to our offer?

No matter how well you position your offer, usually a third amount of people who would be interested are going to be sitting on the fence. Urgency is that genuine push used to get up to half of those fence sitters to buy.

A good headline should aim to accomplish the following 3 things:

- Calls out the target audience by name

- Offers attractive solution to a desperate problem

- Creates compelling intrigue to prod further investigation

Unfortunately, we can't call out every single prospect by their actual name so the best thing to do is to focus on a specific highly targeted segment of any audience that we go after.

The simplest way you can IMPROVE a headline is to be more specific with whom it targets. HINT: target the most profitable segment of a niche!

In other words, you should focus on the most profitable segment of the audience that you're going after and write a headline that would call them out by name. Calling people out by their name only gets their attention so the second part of your headline should offer a solution to their problem.

But as you know, not all solutions are created equal! The better solution you offer, the better is your headline. Here's what makes the solutions attractive:

Instant Gratification - people prefer results now as opposed to later. So if you can promise to solve a problem much faster than what's normally accepted, that would be great.

Believability - how many times have you read a headline that had no credibility whatsoever because of the outrageous claims it was making? The headline has to be believable.

Ease - after reading the headline, you have to make the prospect think that is going to be easy for him to continue on than to leave the page.

Simplicity - don't mention the word "steps" in your headline. People don't want steps, they want a system because too many steps make it look complicated comparing to a system which represents the simplicity of it.

Convenience - the headline has to convince them that it does not take much effort and it is convenient for them to read the sales copy now instead of putting it off for later.

Redemption - how this can help the prospects by reading on to get back at somebody or something or prove somebody or something wrong. This one is not as generally applicable as the rest of them but can be used occasionally.

Final part, **compelling intrigue** - curiosity is a very powerful motivator. What if you said this: "Do you want to know a 13 word sentence from an article published in 1958 that immediately doubled the value of my copy writing skills the first time I used it?" I bet the copy writing prospects would be interested. That's the power of curiosity!

Your headline should go about how you can make this so interesting by not revealing something just yet, just hinting at it to get the person to read on because they have to know the answer.

You should always **TEST** at least two headlines at the very least. This is probably the most important thing thus far. You can have two very good headlines but sometimes there is no way to know which one will work better. Even after you see that one of them is converting better than the other, you still may not know the reason why is that happening. Sometimes you just can't control what is going to happen next, that's why you should always test.

The most neglected thing in any internet marketing business is **SPLIT TESTING** because it takes too long to set up, it takes too long to create the tests and it takes too long to validate the tests.

But if you use the right software, it will take you only five minutes to set it up and five minutes to create two different versions by taking version A, copy and paste the exact same thing for version B and only rewrite the headline. So the total possible time for split testing would be ten minutes, 5 minutes to set up the software that would do the tracking and five minutes to create two different versions.

In order to validate your tests, each page should get at least 300 unique visitors ideally in a short period of time to draw any useful data from the split tests.

Here's a tip that will help you improve your split testing technique and make money in the same time. Contact product owners and offer to split test their sales copy in exchange for 20 percent of any additional sales you bring in. So the product owner is only paying you out of all the extra profit that he would otherwise never made, a small fraction of 20 percent.

Think about it! Some people are generating $1,000 a day without running any split tests. You come in and create a few tests that get them to $2,000 a day. That means you get paid $200 every day while that offer is still running!

Now that you've learned all these great tips on headlines, you should start applying them immediately and go back and rewrite or split test your previous headlines for sales copy, squeeze page, email messages or blog posts.

So we discussed the headline so far but the headline does not sell a single thing! It only gets the prospect to the offer and the offer makes them decide yes or no! The best product in the world will not make a sale if it's not positioned correctly.

Perception of value is the name of the game. People can only measure value accurately only after they gave you their money and got the product. They can't do it before. So for good or bad, it's all about perception of value.

With the right techniques, you can even make something that's horrible have a high perception of value. Regardless of how good or bad the product is, it's all about how you position the offer to buy the product.

Now nobody is suggesting that you do that with horrible products, I'm just saying that you could make it profitable in the short term but you'll probably lose money in the long run. It's not a good long term strategy.

So if you have a great product, you also have to make sure that is perceived as a high value product. To do that you can just focus on three things:

1. Guarantees - make the guarantee of the product better than 90 percent of other guarantees your audience sees. How about a guarantee that goes like this: "Get my product, randomly open it to any page, read for just ten minutes then stop. If you already don't feel like you've got your money back from what you invested in this product today, then I INSIST you contact me directly at this email right here and I will cheerfully give you every penny of your purchase back because I only like to have customers who are happy with their investment today! You risk nothing and you gain everything when you sign up right now!"

2. Bonuses - what are the things you can add to the offer that cost you little time or money but dramatically increase the value of the offer? Well you could go to somebody that has a complimentary product which sells for $97 and ask how much would it cost you to license that product from them. You purchase the license then take their complimentary product, bundle it together with your offer and sell them for the same price of $97 combined, when each would be normally purchased separately for $97. This is just one example of the application of the technique.

3. Aesthetics - make your offer instantly attractive at a mere glance. It does not mean that you need to have the fanciest graphics around. It could just mean that is easy to read or that it stands out and it's simple to consume. In general, having a couple graphics for a graphical layout of the offer is usually a very good idea and it could cost you only 5 dollars on Fiverr to have it done.

Most people who attempt to create copy for themselves or for others:

- Have boring guarantees.

- Lackluster positioning of offer

- You probably cringe rather than feel favorable just by glancing at their offer.

How many do this? Four out of five professional copywriters don't even focus on this stuff because they don't know or they just don't realize how important it is.

By knowing all this stuff, you have a great advantage over others and you can be a lot more effective with your marketing efforts now.

The final piece of the puzzle is **URGENCY**. Even if you write a great headline and position your offer properly, you'll still have some people sitting on the fence whether to purchase or not. Think about this: if the offer is always available and there is no penalty for delaying on taking action and getting the offer then what's the incentive?

There is none! You can sell without urgency but you won't sell a lot.

Mediocre letters neglect it, good letters use it superficially; great letters are BUILT ON IT! So many dead info products can be resuscitated and brought back to life just by adding urgency to them! You could use this as an opportunity to start making money in less than a week. You could for example take an offer, update a few things, re-release it as a special updated version with a time limited discount to celebrate the update. You can make a lot of money helping people re-launch their existing products and add urgency to them.

Don't use urgency in a superficial way and don't lie to people by telling them that they should buy today because the price will increase tomorrow unless you're actually planning to increase it at the mentioned date. Don't say that there are only 20 copies left and when the customer comes back in a week to the offer, he can see that the same amount of copies is still available for purchase. You're shooting yourself in the foot if you're doing it like this because you'll lose a customer for life. It's legally, morally and profitably wrong!!!

Instead, there are ethical ways to use urgency that increases short term conversion and long term profits. Here's the biggest secret behind them: design or "cherry pick" offers that are "inherently urgent!" That's the big secret behind every successful copywriter! The offers that are absolutely urgent like for example someone opens up a coaching program for only 25 students because he can only handle that many at once.

That makes the offer inherently scarce because it's built to be urgent from necessity. You need to build urgency into the offer itself. That would make your life infinitely easier when it comes the time to sell.

Conclusion:

1. If you develop an efficient system for creating and testing headlines
2. If you figured out how to present an offer in the most attractive way while delivering on it!
3. If you created a sense of loss for each passing moment people who saw the offer delayed on getting it...

You will be WEALTHY because nothing gets sold until the copy gets created! Now that you know this, you can create killer copy for yourself or your clients.

Final Words

Congratulations! You've made it to the end! I hope you enjoyed this book and it does mean a lot to me that you have taken the time to read the information I have provided for you.

You've already shown your commitment to learn. But remember, true knowledge is applied knowledge.

So what's my motivation? What do I want?

I want you apply it, change your life, and pay it forward by helping others by sharing these tips and resources with them.

The first way to pay it forward is by writing a review of this book to let others know of the benefits you've got from it.

This will not only help others, but it is incredibly rewarding for me to know how much my work has benefited others as well as learning any ways I can improve.

Other Books Written by Ioan Draniciar

How I Became Vegetarian: Rational Answers to Why Do People Become Vegetarians

Football Mindset Development; A Real Beginner's Guide To Doing What It Takes To Get In The Right Mind Frame To Play Good Football

www.ingramcontent.com/pod-product-compliance
Lightning Source LLC
Chambersburg PA
CBHW051533240526
45471CB00019B/1324